CONTENTS

PLANTS AND ANIMALS

Revised

Flower Power! ....4 ☐

Super Senses ....6 ☐

Revolting Rubbish ....8 ☐

It's Alive! ....10 ☐

Cool Classification ....12 ☐

Sense Investigation ....14 ☐

HUMANS

Revised

Healthy Eating ....16 ☐

Rattle Those Bones...18 ☐

Tremendous Teeth ....20 ☐

Body Investigation ....22 ☐

MATERIALS

	Revised
Mighty Materials 24	☐
Floating and Sinking 26	☐
Which Material? 28	☐
Changing States 30	☐
State Investigation 32	☐

PHYSICAL PROCESSES

	Revised
It's Electric! 34	☐
Sensational Sound 36	☐
Feel The Force 38	☐
Lighten Up 40	☐
Scary Shadows 42	☐
Light Investigation 44	☐

TEST, ANSWERS, USEFUL WORDS

Revision Tests 46	☐
Answers 52	☐
Really Useful Words..55	☐

PLANTS AND ANIMALS

FLOWER POWER!

PRECIOUS PARTS

Write down the correct parts of this plant using the words in the box.

- leaf
- stem
- root
- flower

1.
2.
3.
4.

HARD AT WORK

Match the parts of the plant to the job they do.

a Makes food for the plant.

b Holds the plant in the soil.

c Carries water and goodness around the plant.

d Attracts insects.

1.
2.
3.
4.

Flowers are my favourite part because they are so pretty.

I like the roots best, because they are down there in the mud!

4

PICTURE THIS

Draw the part of the plant described under each box.

1. Holds the plant in the soil.
2. Makes food for the plant.
3. Attracts insects.
4. Carries water and goodness around the plant.

THE COMPLETE PLANT

Draw a picture of a plant in this box. Then add the labels yourself!

top tip
Have a look at a plant in your garden or the park. See if you can name all of the different parts.

PLANTS AND ANIMALS

PLANTS AND ANIMALS

FAMOUS FIVE

What are our five senses? Write them here.

1 _____
2 _____
3 _____
4 _____
5 _____

SUPER SENSES

WHICH PART?

Draw a line to match the sense to the correct part of the body.

1 hearing   2 seeing   3 feeling   4 tasting   5 smelling

Pooh! What's that smell?

A PART TO PLAY

Label this picture with the correct sense. Use the words in the box to help you.

| hearing | seeing | feeling | tasting | smelling |

1. _____
2. _____
3. _____
4. _____
5. _____

SENSIBLE CHOICE!

1. Which sense do you use when you sniff a flower?
2. Which sense do you use when you enjoy a cream cake?
3. Which sense do you use when you stroke a soft cat?
4. Which sense do you use when you listen to music?
5. Which sense do you use when you look at a sunset?

If you had any sense, you'd know...!

top tip
Keep a senses diary through the day. It will help you to realise how much our senses tell us about the world!

PLANTS AND ANIMALS

PLANTS AND ANIMALS

REVOLTING RUBBISH

LITTER FACTS

Write down the answers to these questions.

1 What is litter? _____
_____

2 What is recycling? _____
_____

3 What sorts of objects and materials can be easily recycled?
_____
_____

4 What sort of objects could be re-used instead of thrown away? _____
_____

DANGER!

Rubbish and litter can be dangerous to animals. Draw a line to match the two parts of each sentence to say what can happen.

1 Hedgehogs can get tangled

2 Swans can be poisoned

3 Seals can choke

4 Sea birds can get caught

a ...in the plastic rings that keep cans together in packs.

b ...in fishing line left on the beach.

c ...when they eat lead fishing weights and lures.

d ... when they eat plastic bags floating in the water – they look like jellyfish.

8

RE-USE OR RECYCLE?

Look at this list of things. Which ones can be recycled? And which can be re-used? Draw the things in the correct box.

1. plastic carrier bag
2. cardboard egg box
3. newspaper
4. dairy milk bottle
5. plastic milk bottle
6. drinks can
7. dog food can
8. clear plastic food packaging
9. magazine
10. squash bottle

re-use

recycle

DON'T DROP LITTER!

Draw a poster that tells people not to drop litter. Remember to explain why this is important.

Your room is a tip!

That's utter rubbish!

★ top tip ★
Make sure you re-use carrier bags when you go to the supermarket – it's good for the environment, and it saves money, too!

PLANTS AND ANIMALS

PLANTS AND ANIMALS

LIFE PROCESSES

Write down the seven processes that tell us things are alive.

1 _____
2 _____
3 _____
4 _____
5 _____
6 _____
7 _____

IT'S ALIVE!

ALIVE OR NOT ALIVE?

Draw a circle around the things that are alive.

ALIVE OR ONCE ALIVE?

Alive or once alive? Draw a circle around the things that were alive once, but not now.

DEAD OR ALIVE?

Draw four things that are alive in the butterfly shape. Then draw two things that were once alive in the fossil shape.

"Sam's alive – he eats enough!"

"And you don't?"

top tip
It's difficult to see the seven processes happening in a plant. They dont walk about. But they do move! They grow towards the light, for example.

PLANTS AND ANIMALS

COOL CLASSIFICATION

SORTING ANIMALS AND PLANTS

Help to classify these things by writing animal or plant under them.

1
2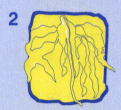
3
4

5
6
7
8

SORTING BUGS AND BIRDS

Bug or bird? Draw the bugs in the box labelled bugs and the birds in the box labelled birds.

bugs | birds

SORTING FEATHERS AND FUR

Fur or feathers? Write fur or feathers in the boxes below each picture.

1

2

3

4

5

6

7

8

YOUR TURN

List the ways you could sort these animals into two groups. An example has been done for you.

Butterfly ladybird spider dragonfly blackbird cat horse rabbit

Things that fly/things that dont fly

Sherbet and chocolate could be in the same set, because they are both types of sweet.

Or they could be in the same set because I've just eaten them both...

top tip
When you are sorting anything – look for what is the same and what is different about the things you are sorting. It will help you to put them into groups.

PLANTS AND ANIMALS

SENSE INVESTIGATION

PLANTS AND ANIMALS

TOUCH

Feel and explore surfaces and textures with your fingers. Then write the words you can think of to describe them here.

_____
_____
_____
_____
_____

SMELL

_____ _____
_____ _____
_____ _____
_____ _____

14

TASTE

How many different tastes can you find? Describe your tastes here.

_____ _____
_____ _____
_____ _____
_____ _____

HEAR

What different sounds can you hear? Describe them here.

_____ _____
_____ _____
_____ _____
_____ _____
_____ _____

SEE

What are the most interesting things you can see? Describe them here.

_____ _____
_____ _____
_____ _____
_____ _____
_____ _____

PLANTS AND ANIMALS

★ top tip ★
Always be careful when you taste something. Check with an adult that it is safe to eat.

HUMANS

HEALTHY EATING

WHICH IS HEALTHIER?

Tick the healthier meal from each pair.

1 Fried egg and chips? ☐ OR Egg salad sandwich? ☐
2 Baked potato and cottage cheese salad? ☐ OR Fish and chips? ☐
3 Fried breakfast? ☐ OR Pasta with tomato sauce? ☐
4 Scrambled egg on wholemeal toast? ☐ OR Takeaway pizza? ☐
5 Tuna salad with boiled new potatoes? ☐ OR Pie and mash? ☐

RIGHT OR WRONG?

Look at these sentences. Write **T** in the box if they are true and **F** if they are false.

1 We do not need to eat lots of fruit and vegetables. ☐
2 We need plenty of sleep. ☐
3 Sugary drinks are good for you so drink lots. ☐
4 We should eat as many sweets as we can every day to exercise our teeth. ☐
5 We should take exercise, including running about and playing games, to keep healthy. ☐

★ top tip ★
Remember – no food is 'bad', but you need to eat a balanced diet with lots of different foods to stay healthy.

I eat lots of fruit, so I get lots of vitamins!

LOVELY LUNCHES

Look back at the three tasks you have done on healthy eating. Use what you have learned to draw a healthy lunch here.

WHAT'S THEIR JOB?

Draw a line to match the foods to the jobs they do.

pasta

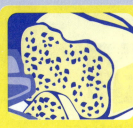
cereals and bread

cheese, nuts and milk

fruit and vegetables

1 Vitamins and fibre

2 Help us to grow and heal when we are hurt

3 Give us fibre, which helps us to digest our food

4 Gives us energy to run and play

If you ate lots of sticky jaw toffee, I'd get lots of peace...

HUMANS

FIND THOSE BONES!

Write the correct labels on the skeleton. Use the words in the box to help you.

- backbone (spine)
- skull
- ribs
- pelvis
- kneecap

1. _____
2. _____
3. _____
4. _____
5. _____

RATTLE THOSE BONES

NAME THEIR JOB

Write down the answers to these questions.

1 Why do we need bones? _____
_____

2 What does our skull protect? _____

3 What are the bones called that protect our soft insides, like our lungs? _____

4 What is the bone called that runs in a line up our backs?
_____

5 Why do we need muscles?
_____

BONES AND MUSCLES

Complete each sentence by writing in the correct word from the box.

floppy   tighten   move   bones   muscles   protect

If we did not have _____, we would be all _____! Bones help us to stand up and _____. They _____ the soft parts of our bodies, like our brains. _____ help our bones to move. When I bend my arm, the muscles _____ up and help to pull the bones where I want them to go.

TRUE OR FALSE?

Tick the statements that are true.

1 The name of the bone that protects the brain is the skull.
2 Our kneecaps are the bones that protect our heart and lungs.
3 Bones support my body. Without them, I would be all stiff!
4 Bones and muscles work together to help me move.
5 There are no bones in my arms.
6 Bones support my body. Without them, I would be all floppy!

Look! I'm a wobbly jelly, I have no bones!

Are you sure it's not your brain that's missing?

top tip
If you bend your knee, you can feel the muscles and bones moving!

TREMENDOUS TEETH

HUMANS

WHAT'S THEIR JOB?

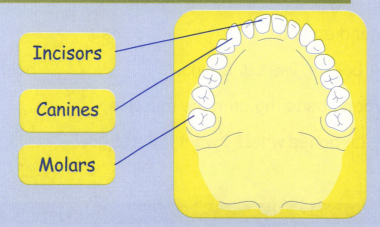

- Incisors
- Canines
- Molars

Write down the job each type of tooth does.

1. The pointed teeth are called canines.
   They are for _____.

2. The teeth at the front are called incisors.
   They are for _____.

3. The teeth at the back are called molars.
   They are for _____.

WHICH IS WHICH?

Draw the right tooth in the boxes to match the job they do!

HEALTHY HABITS

What should you do to keep your teeth healthy? Tick the right answer:

1 Eat lots of sweets.
2 Drink lots of sugary drinks.
3 Visit the dentist twice a year for check-ups.
4 Clean your teeth twice a day.
5 Eat raw vegetables.
6 Do not drink too many sugary drinks.

TRUE OR FALSE

Look at these sentences. Write **T** next to the ones you think are true and **F** next to the ones that are false.

1 Eating lots of sweets is good for your teeth.
2 You should never brush your teeth because you might hurt them.
3 The big teeth at the front of your mouth are called molars.
4 Guinea pigs have long front teeth called incisors.
5 Canines are used for grinding food.

I like going to the dentist – I get a sticker!

I like going HOME from the dentist!

top tip
Wash your hands, then feel your teeth. Now try to find the molars, incisors and canines in your mouth!

HUMANS

BODY INVESTIGATION

MAKE A SKELETON THAT MOVES!

You need these things:

    Tracing or baking paper (or even thin printer paper)
    Pencil
    Card
    Paper clips
    Scissors
    Split pins (which you can get from a newsagents or stationers)

1. Using the tracing paper and pencil, trace the parts of the skeleton on page 23.

2. Use a paper clip to attach the tracing paper to a piece of card – packaging is fine.

3. Cut out the pieces of card. Then join them together with split pins.

4. Make your skeleton move! Bend your arm at the elbow, then bend your skeleton's arm. You could echo the movements you make to explain to somebody how your skeleton works!

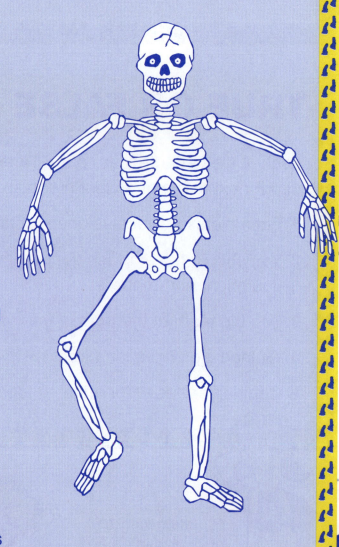

HUMANS

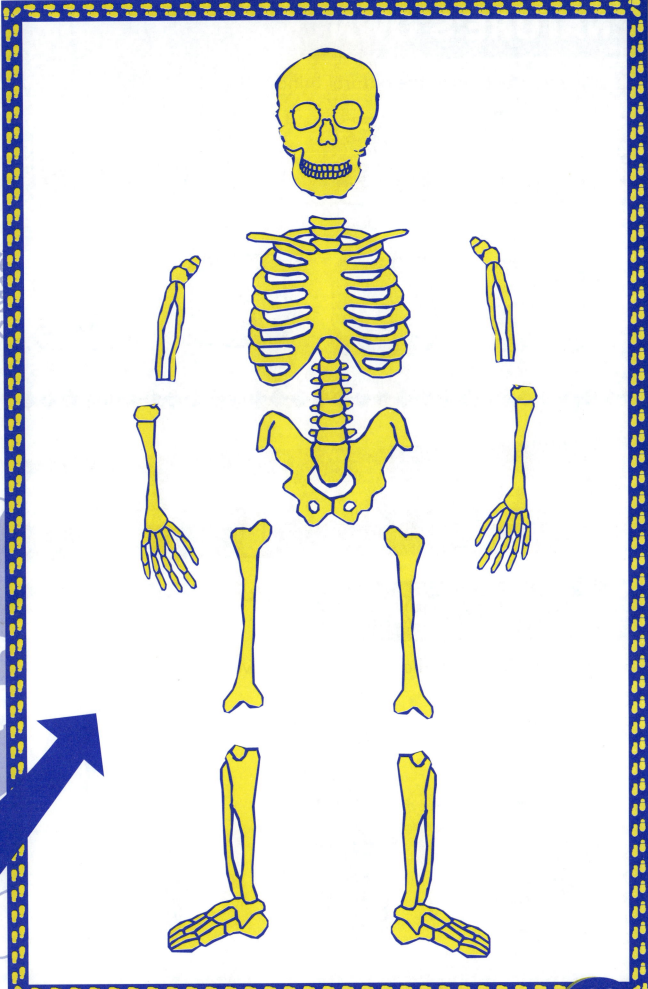

23

MATERIALS

NATURE'S OWN

Draw a circle around the natural things.

1
2
3
4
5
6
7
8

MIGHTY MATERIALS

PEOPLE POWER

Draw a circle around the materials that have been made by people.

1
2
3
4
5
6

MATERIALS

WHERE DOES IT COME FROM?

Draw a line to match the material to where it came from. For example, a pillow can be filled with feathers, so the pillow is joined to the feather. Now try the rest!

SORTING MATERIALS

Draw three natural things in the leaf outline. Then draw three things made by people in the outline of the bag.

I like my leather jacket – naturally, I look cool in it!

I like my feather pillow.

★top tip★
How many natural materials can you find in your house? Make a list.

25

FLOATING AND SINKING

WILL IT FLOAT?

Which things opposite float? Draw the things you choose in the boat shape below.

SINK OR FLOAT?

Draw a line to match the first half of each sentence to the second half, so they make sense.

1 Some things float

2 A pebble would

3 Things float when they are

4 A stone sinks because it is

5 A matchstick would float,

a ...heavy for its size.

b ...light for their size.

c ...but a nail would sink.

d ...and others sink.

e ...sink, but a plastic cup would float.

WILL IT SINK?

Draw a circle round the things that will sink.

MAKE IT FLOAT!

How could you make a ball of plasticine™ float? Why would your idea work?

_____
_____
_____
_____
_____
_____
_____

I love floating in the sea.

I love pretending to be a shark!

★ top tip ★
Find out about how boats float. Now try find out something about the Plimsole line!

MATERIALS

SOFT OR HARD?

Look at these things. Draw the soft ones in the teddy shape. Then draw the hard ones in the rock shape.

WHICH MATERIAL?

SMOOTH OR ROUGH?

Smooth or rough? Write rough underneath the pictures of rough objects and smooth under the pictures of smooth objects.

1. _____ 2. _____ 3. _____ 4. _____ 5. _____

CAN YOU SEE THROUGH IT?

Draw a circle around materials that are transparent (see through).

WHAT IS IT MADE FROM?

Draw a line from the materials to the object you can make from it.

1 plastic   2 fur fabric   3 wood   4 fabric   5 stone

teddy   door   wall   lunchbox   skirt

"My favourite teddy is made out of soft fur fabric."

"My favourite toy is a huge plastic crocodile!"

★ **top tip** ★

Remember, material means what something is made from – not just the stuff clothes are made from!

MATERIALS

CHANGING STATES

MATERIALS

WHAT STATE IS IT?

What state are these things? Sort them into solid, liquid or gas. Write **S**, **L** or **G** in the correct boxes.

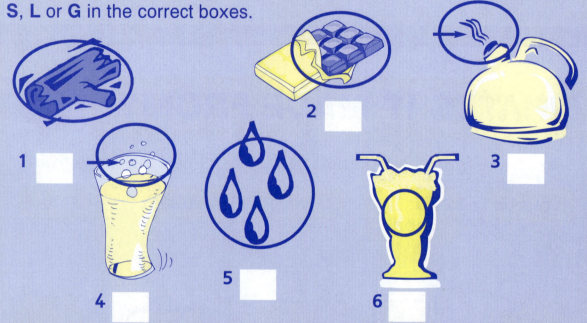

SOLID, LIQUID OR GAS?

Are the things circled in blue, solid, liquid or gas? Write **S**, **L** or **G**.

REVERSIBLE CHANGES

Draw a circle round the changes that are reversible (the things which can be changed and changed back to their original state).

IRREVERSIBLE CHANGES

Tick the box that describes changes that are irreversible (the things cannot change back to their original state).

1 steam coming from pan
2 paper burning
3 cake being baked
4 pancake being fried
5 ice freezing

top tip
Next time you eat a cake – or make one – think about how the ingredients have changed. Make a list of any that can be changed back.

MATERIALS

STATE INVESTIGATION

CRISPIE CAKES

Make some crispie cakes. Yes, it's cookery, but it also shows you how changes of state can be made. You will need an adult to help you, because this task involves handling things that are hot.

I never realised science could be so tasty!

WHAT YOU NEED

You need these things:
A block of chocolate
Crispie breakfast cereal
A bowl that can go in the microwave
A spoon
Cake cases

WHAT TO DO

Break the chocolate into the bowl. Then melt it in the microwave. REVERSIBLE CHANGE ALERT! Chocolate has changed from a *solid* to a *liquid*.

Mix the crispie cereal into the liquid chocolate.

Spoon the mixture into the cake cases and leave in a cool place to set. REVERSIBLE CHANGE ALERT! Chocolate has changed from a *liquid* back to a *solid*.

TIP: You could try making chocolate-coated fruits too – grapes and strawberries are particularly yummy!

MATERIALS

top tip
You can add mini marshmallows or raisins to the mix to make the cakes extra-tasty!

PHYSICAL PROCESSES

IT'S ELECTRIC

WHICH ONES USE ELECTRICITY?

Draw a circle around the things that use electricity.

BATTERY OR MAINS?

Battery or mains electricity? Tick the things that use electricity from a socket in the wall (mains electricity).

34

SOUND SOURCES

Draw a circle round the things that use electricity to make sounds.

MATCH IT UP

Draw a line to match the beginning of each sentence to the second half, so they make sense.

1 Mains electricity

2 Electricity can be used to make heat, like

3 Torches use

4 Electricity can be used to make light,

5 Never poke anything in an electric socket

a ...lovely warm electric fires.

b ...electricity from batteries.

c ...is the type we get from sockets in the wall.

d ...because it can be dangerous!

e ...like the light we get from lamps.

PHYSICAL PROCESSES

top tip
Never open or burn a battery. The chemicals inside can hurt you.

Have you seen my torch?

No, I can't find it, because it's too dark...

35

SOUNDS GOOD!

Now look at these sentences. Tick the ones that are true.

1 Sound travels in invisible waves through the air. ☐
2 We can see sound waves. ☐
3 We hear things as sound enters our ears. ☐
4 We hear things as sound enters our noses. ☐
5 Things sound loudest the closer we are to the thing making the noise. ☐
6 Things sound loudest the further away we are from the thing making the noise. ☐

SENSATIONAL SOUND

SAFE SOUNDS

Write down the answers to these questions.

1 Why should you never poke things in your ears?
　
2 What noises might you hear in a town?
　
3 What things make LOUD sounds? Write down four.
　
4 What things make QUIET sounds? Write down four.
　
5 Why do people wear ear protectors when they are using loud machinery?
　

PHYSICAL PROCESSES

HEAR HEAR

Circle the place you think the dog sounds loudest.

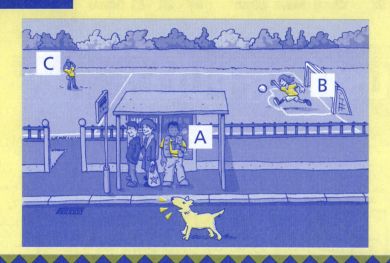

LOUD OR QUIET?

Go on a sounds walk – in your home if you are alone, or outside if you are with a grown-up. Make a list of all the things you hear. Mark the loud things with **L** and the quiet sounds with **Q**.

_____   _____
_____   _____
_____   _____
_____   _____
_____   _____
_____   _____
_____   _____

PHYSICAL PROCESSES

I like LOUD noises!

Must be why you like me!

★ top tip ★
Be careful around loud noises. They can damage your hearing!

FEEL THE FORCE

PUSH OR PULL?

Write Push or Pull in the boxes below each picture to describe the forces.

1
2
3
4
5

GRAVITY

Complete these sentences about gravity by writing in the correct word from the box.

> force   smaller   fall   float   Moon   pulled

1 Gravity is a _____ .

2 Gravity is the force that makes things _____ to the ground when you drop them.

3 Everything is _____ towards the centre of the Earth by gravity.

4 Without gravity, things would _____ about!

5 Gravity is not as strong on the _____ as on the Earth.

6 Gravity is not as strong on the Moon because the Moon is much _____ than the Earth.

38

PHYSICAL PROCESSES

FRICTION

Which has more friction?

1 walking on *wet tiles* ☐
 or *dry tiles*? ☐

2 walking on an *icy path* ☐
 or a *dry path*? ☐

3 sledging on a *snowy hill* ☐
 or on a *hill with no snow*? ☐

4 skidding on an *icy playground* ☐
 or a *dry playground*? ☐

5 rubbing together *dry hands* ☐
 or *wet hands*? ☐

6 rubbing together *wet hands* ☐
 or *soapy wet hands*? ☐

WHICH FORCE?

1 Which force stops us from slipping?
 _____

2 Which force makes things fall when we drop them?
 _____

3 Why are we more likely to slip on a wet floor than a dry floor?
 _____

4 Which force makes our hands warm up when we rub them together on a cold day?
 _____

I wonder why Mum says there's always friction when we are together?

It's because you're always rubbing me up the wrong way!

★ **top tip** ★
Have a go at rubbing your hands together 1. when they are dry 2. when they are wet 3. when they are wet and soapy. How do they feel different to each other?

39

SOURCES OF LIGHT

Draw a circle around the things that are soures of light.

1  2  3  4

5  6  7  8

LIGHTEN UP

LOVELY LIGHT

Look at these sentences. Tick the ones that are true.

1 Light travels in straight lines.

2 Light bends around objects that get in its way.

3 We see things when light bounces off them and into our eyes.

4 A fire is a source of light.

5 A candle is a source of light.

6 A torch is not a source of light.

7 A sequin is not a source of light, but it is shiny, because it reflects light.

40

LET IT GLOW!

Look at this picture of a bedroom. Now draw a circle around all of the sources of light you can see.

CAN YOU SEE IT!

Draw the beam of light to show how the cat can see the mouse.

top tip
Remember, shiny things are not sources of light. They just reflect it, like the Moon!

PHYSICAL PROCESSES

I don't like the dark much, so I like sources of light.

I like creeping around in the dark, so I can make you jump!

41

SCARY SHADOWS

SHADOWS

Draw a line to match the first and second parts of the sentences about shadows so they make sense!

1. Your shadow is made
2. Light travels in
3. Shadows are short and fat at midday
4. Shadows show us
5. Shadows are longest

a ...when the Sun is high overhead.
b ...straight lines.
c ...in the late afternoon.
d ...where the light has not been able to pass through an object.
e ...because you block the light.

SHADOW PUPPETS

Can you explain how the girl is making the bunny shadow on the wall?

_____
_____
_____
_____
_____
_____

CHANGING SHADOWS

Look at the shadow of this cat. Match the labels to the correct picture.

a The Sun is overhead, high in the sky, so the cat's shadow is short and fat.

b The Sun is low in the sky in the late afternoon, so the cat's shadow is tall and thin.

WHERE'S THE SUN?

Draw the Sun in three places: at sunrise, midday and sunset. Write the words as labels under each Sun you draw.

I like it when my shadow is tall and thin!

It's amazing, considering how much you eat!

★ top tip ★
Check out how shadows move through the day. Chalk round a shadow at midday, and again at about 4pm. How have things changed?

PHYSICAL PROCESSES

LIGHT INVESTIGATION

MAKE A SIMPLE SUNDIAL

You need these things:

Card (and something round to draw round like a teaplate)

Scissors

Pencil

Watch

Pen

WHAT TO DO

1. Draw around the tea plate onto your card.
2. Cut out the circle.
3. Push the pencil through the centre of your circle (you can find the centre by drawing lines that cross through the middle of the circle).
4. Stick the pencil in the ground, with the circle attached. It should be in a very sunny spot.
5. Mark the position of the shadow of the pencil on each hour (look at your watch). Draw a line and label it with the time.

The next day, you won't need a watch, because you have a sundial!

TIP: You can make a weather proof sundial from plastic packaging and marking the hours in waterproof felt pen.

PHYSICAL PROCESSES

REVISION TEST

1 Draw a picture of the part of the plant next to the description of the job it does:

a Attracts insects with its scent and colour.

b Holds the plant in the ground.

c Makes food using sunlight.

2 Draw the parts of the body we use for each sense:

hearing   seeing   touching   tasting   smelling

3 List six pieces of rubbish that could be recycled.

a _____

b _____

c _____

d _____

e _____

f _____

4 Draw four things that are alive in the flower shape below.

5 Sort these creatures into the two groups below:

| robin | dog | penguin | butterfly | horse | crab |

can fly

cannot fly

REVISION TEST

6 Tick the foods in each pair that are the healthier choices?

   a apples ☐
       OR
       apple pie ☐

   c cheese pasties ☐
       OR
       cubes of cheese ☐

   b orange juice ☐
       OR
       orange squash ☐

   d milk ☐
       OR
       cola ☐

7 Draw a line to match the bones to the part of the body they protect.

   a heart and lungs   **1** skull

   b brain   **2** pelvis

   c kidneys   **3** ribs

8 Fill in the answers.

   a Write down the teeth that are used for grinding food.

   b Write down the teeth that a dog uses for tearing meat.

   c Write down the teeth that a rabbit uses for chopping carrots.

9 Draw three natural objects in the basket shape below.

10 Make a list of six things that would sink in a bowl of water.

a _____

b _____

c _____

d _____

e _____

f _____

11 Choose the best material to make each object, then join them with a line.

a metal   1 door

b wood   2 lunchbox

c glass   3 comic

d plastic   4 window

e paper   5 lorry

12 Solid, liquid or gas? Write S, L or G to explain the state of these things:

a metal ☐   c apple ☐   e orange juice ☐   g air ☐

b milk ☐   d steam ☐   f wood ☐   h petrol ☐

13 Tick the things that can be changed back to the way they started.

a An egg that has been boiled. ☐

b A meringue that has been cooked. ☐

c Coal that has been burned. ☐

d Ice that has melted. ☐

14 Tick the items that are a source of light.

REVISION TEST

a Moon ☐   g car headlight ☐   m sequins ☐
b fire ☐   h TV (turned on) ☐   n computer monitor (turned on) ☐
c mirror ☐   i candle ☐
d Sun ☐   j lamp ☐
e torch ☐   k glitter ☐
f aluminium foil ☐   l window ☐

15 Draw three things that use battery electricity.

16 Where do you think the radio sounds the loudest? Mark the place with a circle.

50

17

a Write down the force that makes things fall to the ground when they are dropped.

___

b Write down the force that stops us from slipping over.

___

18 Explain below how the girl sees the butterfly.

___

19 Draw the shadow of a car in the following times:

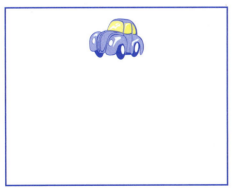

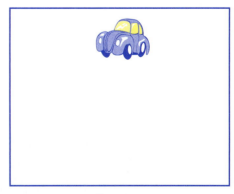

a midday and the Sun is overhead, high in the sky.

b when the Sun is low in the sky in the late afternoon.

ANSWERS

PLANTS AND ANIMALS

Pages 4–5
Precious parts
  1 flower 2 leaf 3 stem 4 root
Hard at work
  1 d 2 a 3 c 4 b
Picture this

  1 root   2 leaf   3 flower   4 stem

The complete plant

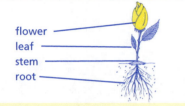

flower
leaf
stem
root

Pages 6–7
Famous five
  In any order: seeing, hearing, feeling, tasting, smelling.
Which part?

  1 hearing 2 seeing 3 feeling 4 tasting 5 smelling

A part to play
  1 hearing   4 seeing
  2 smelling   5 tasting
  3 feeling

Sensible choice
  1 smell 2 taste 3 touch 4 hearing
  5 sight

Pages 8–9
Litter facts
  1 Litter is rubbish left lying around.
  2 Recycling is taking glass, paper, cans and sometimes plastic to be re made into other useful objects.
  3 paper, glass, cans
  4 A variety of answers – carrier bags, yoghurt pots to grow seeds; plastic bottles cut in half and the top turned upside down as a funnel etc.

Danger!
  1 a 2 c 3 d 4 b

Re-use or recycle
  re-use: 1, 2, 5 and 8
  recycle: 3, 4, 6, 7, 9 and 10

Don't drop litter
  Poster containing info about the dangers of litter.

Pages 10–11
Life processes
  breathe
  get rid of waste
  have babies
  feed
  move
  feel things
  grow and change

Alive or not alive?

Alive or once alive?

Dead or alive?
  Variety of answers such as:
  in butterfly: cat, mouse, moth, grass
  in fossil: pressed flower, dried corn, ammonite

Pages 12–13
Sorting animals and plants
  1 animal 2 plant   3 animal 4 plant
  5 animal 6 animal 7 plant   8 plant

Sorting bugs and birds
  bugs: worm, spider, ladybird, snail
  birds: penguin, owl, swan, turkey

Sorting feathers and fur
  fur: 1, 4, 5 and 6   feathers: 2, 3, 7 and 8

Your turn
  Variety of answers – bugs/not bugs, eats plants/eats other creatures, has 4 legs/has more than 4 legs.

Pages 14–15
  Child should fill in the things they have seen/heard/tasted/felt/touched.

52

HUMANS

Pages 16–17
Which is healthier?
1. sandwich
2. baked potato and salad
3. pasta
4. scrambled egg
5. tuna salad and potatoes

Right or wrong?
1 F   2 T   3 F   4 F
5 T

Lovely lunches
Any healthy balanced meal.

What's their job?
pasta = 4
cereals and bread = 3
cheese, nuts and milk = 2
fruit and vegetables = 1

Pages 18–19
Find those bones
1. skull
2. ribs
3. backbone
4. pelvis
5. kneecap

Name their job
1. to support our bodies; to help us move; to protect soft bits like our brains and hearts
2. brain
3. ribs
4. backbone or spine
5. muscles work with our bones to help us move

Bones and muscles
If we did not have **bones**, we would be all **floppy**! Bones help us to stand up and **move**. They **protect** the soft parts of our bodies, like our brains. **Muscles** help our bones to move. When I bend my arm, the muscles **tighten** up and help to pull the bones where I want them to go.

True or false
1 T   2 F   3 F   4 T
5 F   6 T

Pages 20–21
What's their job?
1. canines for tearing
2. incisors for cutting and biting
3. molars for chewing and grinding

Which is which?

1 incisor   2 canine   3 molar

Healthy habits
3, 4, 5 and 6 should be ticked.

True or false
1 F   2 F   3 F   4 T
5 F

Pages 22–23
Body investigation
Check the child follows the instructions to make the skeleton that moves.

MATERIALS

Pages 24–25
Nature's own
2 3 4 5 8

People power
3 5 6

Where does it come from?

Sorting materials
Variety of answers suitable such as feathers, stones, shells (natural) and plastic, polystyrene (made by people).

Pages 26–27
Will it float?
cork, paper boat

Sink or float?
1 d   2 e   3 b   4 a
5 c

Will it sink?
coin, hammer, ball of plasticine

Make it float!
Explanation that by flattening the plastercine™ the water then pushes up on the bottom of it; making a big surface has made the plastercine™ light for its size etc.

Pages 28–29
Soft or hard?
teddy: bunny, bobble hat, pillow
rock: car, spoon, book

Smooth or rough?
rough: 1 and 3   **smooth:** 2 4 5

Can you see through it?
window, glass, fish bowl

What is it made from?
1 lunchbox 2 teddy 3 door 4 skirt 5 wall

Pages 30–31
What state is it?
1 S   2 S   3 G   4 G   5 L   6 L

Solid, liquid or gas?
1 G   2 S   3 L   4 S   5 G

Reversible changes
1 butter   2 chocolate   3 ice

Irreversible changes
2, 3 and 4

Pages 32–33
State investigation
Ensure the child follows the crispy cake recipe.

PHYSICAL PROCESSES

Pages 34–35
Which ones use electricity?
2 kettle, 3 torch, 5 TV and 6 lamp
Battery or mains?
1 radio, 2 Hi-fi, 4 TV and 7 CD player
Sound sources
1 music centre, 3 CD player, 6 TV and 8 radio
Match it up
1 c 2 a 3 b 4 e
5 d

Pages 36–37
Sounds good!
1, 3 and 5 should be ticked.
Safe sounds
Variety of answers suitable.
1 You could damage your ears and your hearing.
2 Variety of answers such as cars, sirens, alarms, buses etc.
3 Variety of answers such as sirens, machinery, motors, explosions etc.
4 Variety of answers such as mouse, leaf falling, bird singing etc.
5 To avoid ear damage.
Hear, hear
answer: A
Loud or quiet?
Variety of answers, ask the child to make a list of quite and loud noises.

Pages 38–39
Push or pull?
push: 1, 2, 3 and 5   pull: 4
Gravity
1 force   4 float
2 fall   5 Moon
3 pulled   6 smaller
Friction
1 dry tiles   4 dry playground
2 dry path   5 dry hands
3 hill with no snow   6 wet hands
Which force?
1 friction
2 gravity
3 less friction – water coats the floor and makes it slippery
4 friction

Pages 40–41
Sources of light

Lovely light
1, 3, 4, 5 and 7
Let it glow

Can you see it?

Pages 42–43
Shadows
1 e 2 b 3 a 4 d
5 c
Shadow puppets
Any reasonable explanation containing the key points that light has been blocked by an opaque object; light travels in straight lines etc.
Changing shadows
1 → b
2 → a
Where's the sun?

sunset   midday   sunrise

Pages 44–45
Light investigation
Check the child follows the instruction to make a sundial.

Pages 46–47 Revision Test
1
2
3 Variety of answers. Glass bottle, jam jar, cat food tin, bean tin, drinks can, newspaper, comic, magazine etc.
4 Variety of answers are correct as long as they are plants and animals.
5 **can fly:** butterfly, robin
  cannot fly: penguin, horse, crab, dog
6 a apples   b orange juice
  c cubes of cheese d milk
7 a 3 b 1 c 2
8 a molars   b canines
  c incisors
9 Variety of answers such as shell, pebble, feather etc.
10 Variety of answers, such as: pebble, stone metal spoon, marble, metal toy car, shell.
11 a 5 b 1 c 4 d 2
   e 3
12 a S b L c S d G
   e L f S g G h L
13 d should be ticked.
14 b, d, e, g, h, i, j and n should be ticked.
15 Variety of answers including toys, torch, portable radios and CD players, TV remote control.
16 Next to mother.
17 a gravity   b friction
18 The light hits the butterfly, bounces off and enters the girl's eye.
19 a   b

REALLY USEFUL WORDS

PLANTS AND ANIMALS

Alive If something is alive, it goes through seven processes. It moves, breathes, feeds, makes waste, grows, has babies, feels things.

Canine teeth Sharp, pointy teeth used for tearing food such as meat. Dogs and cats have canine teeth.

Classification The word scientists use when they sort things into groups such as plants and animals.

Flower Part of a plant. It is usually very brightly coloured and smells nice so that it attracts insects.

Leaf Part of a plant. It makes food by using energy from the Sun.

Litter Rubbish. Things we have no use for.

Recycling When materials such as glass and paper are collected and made into new materials, we say it has been recycled.

Re-using When something is used for another purpose instead of being thrown away. An example would be using yoghurt pots to plants seeds.

Root Part of a plant. Roots hold the rest of the plant in the soil.

Stem Part of a plant. It carries water and goodness around the plant.

HUMANS

Backbone Another name for spine. It is the large bone that goes down the centre of the back.

Carbohydrate Gives the body instant energy. Pasta and bread are good sources of carbohydrates.

Fibre Helps us to digest food. Fruit, vegetables, wholemeal bread and cereals are good sources of fibre.

Incisors The teeth used for chopping and shredding food.

Kneecaps The rounded bones on our knees are called kneecaps.

Molars The teeth used for grinding food.

Muscles The fibres attached to our bones. They help us to move.

Pelvis the bony case above our legs that protect the soft bits or 'organs' inside us. If you put your hands on your hips, you are touching your pelvis

Protein Helps our bodies to repair themselves. It is found in foods like nuts and cheese.

HUMANS CONTINUED

Ribs The cage of bones that protect the soft bits or 'organs' inside us, like our hearts and lungs.

Senses We have five of these: hearing, seeing, touching, smelling, tasting are our senses.

Skull The bony case that protects our brain.

Spine Another name for the backbone.

Vitamins Goodness we get from our food. Vitamins are found in fruit and vegetables, and help us to fight things like coughs and colds.

MATERIALS

Gas A gas is a material like oxygen or the air we breathe. It spreads out to fill the space it is in.

Irreversible change Something that cannot be changed back to its original state. Paper (a solid) being burned is an irreversible change. See Reversible change.

Liquid A liquid flows and can be poured. An example would be water.

Materials What things are made from. They can be natural, like wood. Or they can be man-made, like plastic.

Reversible changes A change that can be reversed. For example, ice (a solid) can melt into a liquid and then be frozen again into a solid.

Solid A solid is a material that holds its shape and does not flow like a liquid. An example would be wood.

State Scientists call 'solid', 'liquid' and 'gas' states.

Transparent Things that we can see through. Glass is transparent.

PHYSICAL PROCESSES

Battery A source of electricity. It is used to power things like torches and toys.

Electricity A source of energy. It can be mains electricity (which you get by plugging things into sockets) or from batteries.

Friction Friction is a force that happens when two surfaces rub together. It takes away energy from moving objects and slows them down.

Gravity The force that makes things fall to the ground.

Shadow These are made when light is blocked by an object – such as a person!

Source of light Things that make light such as a candle, an electric light or the Sun.